SANTIAGO

Cheryl Follon was born in Ayrshire, where she grew up. She studied in Glasgow and Dublin. Now she teaches in a further education college in Glasgow, and a good deal of her free time is spent travelling. Her essay on the Mojave Desert was shortlisted for the Shiva Naipaul Memorial Prize for travel writing. She has published three collections with Bloodaxe, *All Your Talk* (2004), *Dirty Looks* (2010) and *Santiago* (2017).

CHERYL FOLLON

Santiago

BLOODAXE BOOKS

ISBN: 978 1 78037 335 5

First published 2017 by
Bloodaxe Books Ltd,
Eastburn,
South Park,
Hexham,
Northumberland NE46 1BS.

www.bloodaxebooks.com
For further information about Bloodaxe titles
please visit our website or write to
the above address for a catalogue.

Supported by
**ARTS COUNCIL
ENGLAND**

Cover design: Neil Astley & Pamela Robertson-Pearce.

Printed in Great Britain by Bell & Bain Limited, Glasgow, Scotland, on
acid-free paper sourced from mills with FSC chain of custody certification.

For my family

CONTENTS

Insomnia 9 | Blood 10 | Brogues 11 | New York 12 | Negativity 13 | Fate 14 | Lightbulb 15 | Couch 16 | Digital Clock Display 17 | Sugar 18 | Sultan 19 | Contrariness 20 | Moth 21 | Manners 22 | Air Con 23 | Novels 24 | Canoeing 25 | Croissant 26 | Boredom 27 | Russian Doll 28 | Grimm Tales 29 | Magnesium 30 | Amulet 31 | Comma 32 | Pineapple 33 | Time Difference 34 | Dutch Cuisine 35 | Airline Food 36 | Ear Canal 37 | Sea Anemone 38 | Netball 39 | Socks 40 | Hanoi 41 | Tree 42 | Snow 43 | Paper Flowers 44 | Crème Caramel 45 | Python 46 | Shyness 47 | Patience 48 | Fame 49 | Geneva 50 | Memories 51 | Pretzel 52 | Loneliness 53 | Making Do 54 | Sculpture 55 | Ripples 56 | Brain 57 | Octopus 58 | Light 59 | Rain 60 | Fire 61 | Istanbul 62 | Anxiety 63 | Luck 64 | TV 65 | Sapphire 66 | Hormones 67 | Iceland 68 | Cartoonist 69 | Water 70 | Shadows 71 | Homesickness 72 | Grasshopper 73 | Knife 74 | Dust Motes 75 | Jealousy 76 | Heartbreak 77 | Fly 78 | Sand 79 | Lion 80 | Surgery 81 | Radio Waves 82 | Butter 83 | Oxygen 84 | Addiction 85 | Forgetfulness 86 | Sleep 87 | Bluebeard 88 | Minneapolis 89 | Wedding 90 | Fashion 91 | Tattoo 92 | Santiago 93 | *Acknowledgements 96* |

INSOMNIA

I took my insomnia down the white hot heat of a two-mile strip of kebabists, ice-cream parlours, waffles, New Balance shoes and gypsy dancing. We got to spend the time together we didn't usually get. We had a waffle and cream and insomnia told me about its plans for the future, its dreams.

BLOOD

Blood's kept busy around the orange TVs, old suede two-
seaters, backgammon boards and teacups at Peter's Market
– everywhere, really. A little more effort required at the
soft grey dust of the old films. Plenty of work at the
hospital. There's not much time for anything else, really,
but blood manages – squeezes in what it can.

BROGUES

A man from Boston got brogues going – after a first-class childhood spent with his feet up on his granny's great expensive cabinets looking at the framed photos of the dead pets. The dead pet photos were all gone, and so was granny's house, but he relived the experience again and again by wrapping the closest he could get to those big cabinets around his feet and he got the brogues going.

NEW YORK

The only way to really understand this city is to do it bit by bit – like snapping the tiny pieces of a massive jigsaw puzzle together, but doing it all with the lights out; or getting dressed at a Salvation Army junk stall, also in the dark, and it all turning out, in the end, immaculate.

NEGATIVITY

Hey, listen! Do you really think I want to stand around doing dishes at five in the morning? Do you really think that I want dinners like salted potatoes out of a tin can, or to go carting two gallons of disinfectant around the place? Would you hear me out now and just listen? Come on: I'm singing you a song.

FATE

Never mind fate – that just wants to make sure it remembers the great lines it's got for a book: 'taking the mad mullah's midnight rust bucket taxi'; '30mph when it's meant to be 130'; 'like being strapped to a washing machine and thrown from a cliff'. Fate just wants to store them all up before something intervenes – that sharp knock at the door by a Mr Mullah the cock-eyed handyman looking for 30 dollars' worth of small change for spare parts.

LIGHTBULB

The essence and brilliance of it fully illuminated when you simply don't have one: sitting in two feet squared of rich pitch black; the sorry pit of five million years of anti-evolution.

COUCH

The couch came in around the seventeenth century, along with that era's French or maybe Spanish writers. They wanted something they could lie on, eat on, work from, even die on. Something they could give orders from, conduct any business from. You might think this is more about the writers, but it is not. This is one hundred per-cent living-breathing couch.

DIGITAL CLOCK DISPLAY

I've many fond memories of this place. Too bad they're all memories.

SUGAR

Some call me fudge, others monster cone. Others launch right in with doughnut or pouring syrup. Others are more creative with their hot stream of sugar sugar puff puff. Yeah, yeah – I get Swiss roll, too. And all of this even though I'd rather just stay at home with my feet up and a nice quiet cup of tea.

SULTAN

A square mile of petting zoo, date palms, glass fountains, lions, peacocks, and still the sultan wanders around smacking a stick through the dead leaves in a fountain and wishing he could just have lunch in the Ol' Kitchenette with the girl from Scotland with the funny accent and the ring of paper flowers in her hair... Be the boy with the scooter who slouches around the pet shop hitting the magic popcorn fountain with a stick.

CONTRARINESS

My girlfriend treats me like dirt, and really enjoys it. She says it's down to her two-way split. She's the kind of girl who says 'as there's no one here to give me oral I gotta read this boring magazine'. Or, 'I'm just so deeply aware of the grave, or maybe just a slave to my big clit'. That's the kind of girl she is – the words *grave* and *clit* in the same sentence. Her two-way split, she says.

MOTH

The mystery and brilliance of the moth is down to its recipe, or *a* recipe. The wacky palette of earth... Browns, blacks, blues, reds, greens, golds... Vermeer painting a jug of wine because it reminded him of his mother, or a large black velvet hat because it reminded him of his father – pure moth. The tones and papers, and oils, too.

MANNERS

The master of the desert and grasslands – kingdom of date and fig and camel, as far as the eye can see – 2,000,000 camels and just as many foot soldiers, camps collapsed and set up 40 miles on. And her – legendary baths, rose oil, flannels of milk, black and white eunuchs, a trail of pink petals falling out behind her while she walks. He was brought up to lead all men, and she was brought up to do the same. On the burning gold of the Eternal Gold Palace the sound of two voices... No, please, let's take my horse; no, I insist – let's take *my* horse...

AIR CON

Air con is not generally needed in boats as the waves of the water are always almost enough to offset or completely cancel out the Dance of the Air Con, or the air con's Aria in D Minor.

NOVELS

When the author writes, 'twenty ice-white snowy owls soothed out of the woods', the reader knows that didn't really happen, and that's the same for 'a string of eight yellow song birds darted in the bathroom window and did figures of eight and loop-the-loops and then went out again, and all this while I stretched out underneath in the bath'. The reader knows this didn't happen – but imagine if it did...

CANOEING

Come on team: fly through this like the big white gull coming through the back window, passing through the kitchen, the hall, both bedrooms, and out through the same window without flexing a wisp of a feather, or bending. Then you'll win it. And they did.

CROISSANT

The most illustrious thing about the croissant is that it came out more or less right the first time – like a miracle.

BOREDOM

So boredom comes with its inbuilt sliding scale (that woman in Hot Wing Grill a four, and that man in the mirrors-and-fluorescent-tube-den Scents for You a seven. The French fish scientist a two, while the Canadian ice hockey player is a nine, and the Dutch woman with the urinary tract infection a three, which is also the same as a nine, but which can be taken as a one, and maybe even a six, etcetera etcetera, yadda yadda yadda).

RUSSIAN DOLL

I was eaten up by worry over the possibility that all I'd inherited from my mother was a moustache; and that was subsumed by worrying about where I'd store my huge blow-up Nessie and double lilo. Then that was subsumed by worrying about who'd win in a fight between a gull and a crow. But it was all subsumed by my love of my scooter. Subsumed, wrapped up – Russian doll tight.

GRIMM TALES

Uncle made that pudding so bittersweet, so cherry, so German, so garlic milk, so knife in the soup, that he could scoop it out and make deep dark forests with it.

MAGNESIUM

So I kept 20,000 servants with the sole purpose of doing nothing more than tickling my feet – but when the magnesium was brought out in its white box no one was allowed to touch it – not even me.

AMULET

I looked everywhere for a sign that you were happy, but I could find nothing; so I looked everywhere for a sign that you were unhappy, but, again, nothing. So I looked everywhere for a sign that you were content, aghast – nope, not a trace. I tried for comfortable, settled, resigned – again, *nada*. So I assumed you were either dead, or maybe so utterly impoverished you were right at the bottom of things, and at that point I suppose I sat back and closed my eyes.

COMMA

The comma's life is a bland affair – not like the brain's pulsing muscle that likes drills and exercises – the verb sent to the end, the exception to the rule. Fits and bursts that keep the brain going, its heel and ankle twisting about in the mud... The comma doesn't need adrenaline, or sport socks – just a little knitting, maybe; or cards.

PINEAPPLE

It's as if the pineapple fell in love with pure instinct itself: rugged and rough on the outside, soft and sweet on the inside – probably pretty ambitious, too.

TIME DIFFERENCE

If you take a piss now the astronomers with their telescopes in Madrid will see you three hours ago.

DUTCH CUISINE

The prince quits laughing at the cow napkins and big clogs and is marvelling at the delicate palate of the Dutch – the barely-there apple; the milk patties; the thin white bread; lemonade bubbles; the slightest hint of parsley – till he wonders if he's even in Holland at all, or a prince.

AIRLINE FOOD

Sluggish blood and pretzel dust come together to make the top line in airline food: a kind of grey doily draped ever so lightly over the senses.

EAR CANAL

The delicate passage of the ear canal – that narrow channel – a Chinese galleon goes down it twisting sails dramatically every few seconds to the left and right... And in the manoeuvres the unmistakable smell of a dusting of cinnamon, hoof protein, oily keratin and more than a hint of freshly fried doughnuts. Even the Chinaman boatman with the permanent scowl smiles a little. Temperate to downright hot – sometimes the thing so dried out they think about calling it the ear *camel*...

SEA ANEMONE

In amongst the two-mile deep acid scrapes, ossifying grit craters, and an odd crosscurrent of green, a single sea-anemone voice: I knew I shouldn't have worn this dress.

NETBALL

It didn't matter that my mother thought I was like something grown in a dark room or that without my glasses I looked like a baby bird with skewed dots for eyes that had fallen out the nest. There was all this but it didn't matter one bit because I found netball, and then it was the mad white blur of fourteen pairs of white socks, ten ponytails, an electric buzz that is team play and makes a dark room a white one with no roof, no ceiling and no walls and two hoops hovering like giant quivering *oms*.

SOCKS

Keep an eye on them: down amongst the toothpaste and the wooden clothes horses, the cut-price bikinis, or shifting around picnic-ware, or the mini chess sets. Even when going for milk it's something like a military operation: maps spread out on the table, paper weights; questioning the man at the desk for possible pit stops and setbacks; who and who not to avoid, detours, short cuts.

HANOI

In the old quarter there is the street of relics, the street of wooden drums, the street of teaspoons, the street of metal coffeepots. Someone wants green tea or jasmine tea and they've put male potency pills in their basket instead, skin-whitening pills. They're going home now to make a coconut cake complete with stray cats and lizards, the street of funeral urns, the street of relics.

TREE

In my youth I dreamed of becoming an actress, but – and not a moment too soon – realised the notion was ridiculous and that I should just be myself.

SNOW

It starts as plinky flecks, then turns to big wet slaps on the window. Snow says, you ever spread a snow blanket down and done algebra under the big snow tree? You got no style, no nothing. A mouth like a giraffe. How come you're scared of turnstiles? Come on, it says, let's play snowball.

PAPER FLOWERS

Just when the hash smokers are going out to shoplift Scotch eggs, and the neighbour is drinking milkshake, paper flowers is making paper flowers – endless strings of the things for an endless cycle of births, deaths and marriages.

CRÈME CARAMEL

The annual crème caramel eating competition is in full
swing: where one man eats his weight in crème caramel
and takes the yellow gold medal.

PYTHON

It's not like I hang around in hotel guests' rooms going through their medical stuff – pessaries, fungal foot cream, mini shaving kits and the rest of it – or I'm getting caught trying on their frocks, or going through their pockets, or setting little traps like toothpaste on the toilet seat. It's not like I'm doing these kinds of things, but if I were – well then...

SHYNESS

Not easy keeping the world's deepest secret; and when even the electronic hand dryer is trying to get it out of you.

PATIENCE

So while you played cock of the walk, striding out and over, it's true I held back and stayed in the shadows where I thought the Renaissance was something served with boiled potatoes and a ciabatta was a fancy shoe. But you didn't realise I was just *familiarising* myself with things...

FAME

I can't decide if I'm trying to wheedle my way into The Savoy with an old receipt for milk, or maybe barter for old milk with my charming ol' tales of my stays at The Savoy.

GENEVA

You can miss someone, but you'll miss them more in Geneva. That city with its little animal graves up the park, and those grey trams coasting slowly over the hills. A lot of concrete. Suliman's Burger and Kebab. A real emptiness. You miss someone more in Geneva, maybe like you are missing emptiness itself.

.

MEMORIES

They come out at night, when it's warm. Once everyone has gone, even the guy who creeps around the park in the leather poncho. They make noises? Maybe. Someone who came back from a late night drinking session at a bar sat up against a wall and said she saw them, but it's unlikely. I mean – the guy in the leather poncho – who's even seen *him*?

PRETZEL

Those two grey-faced billionaires – one of them just sits and nurses an orange juice all day while the other thinks about getting a pretzel but doesn't. All this makes them close – closer than ever really – the way your fingers sit side by side with one another.

LONELINESS

Loneliness didn't start around the time of the craze for building matchstick houses and the Little Mermaid in Denmark, but a long time before both of those. Molluscs even know loneliness, although moss doesn't, and that universal, ubiquitous substance can't even grow around loneliness – not even if it were a small black jewel, or a red one.

MAKING DO

I went to a bar through a fridge door in a florists.

SCULPTURE

Tits and arses in mashed potato, someone else shouted.
No – draw *ellipses* – the circle that's been flattened. The
two came together in Henry Moore as while out drinking
at a bar he overheard it all... Two things melded together
at a pleasing crossroads... Flattened potato – tits...

RIPPLES

The President Elect takes his big ass and green rubber ducks into the bath to sink or swim. To sink or swim into the bath his big green ducks, his rubber ass, the President Elect takes.

BRAIN

Sometimes chopped up and put in ravioli, but most of the time putting rockets into the sky or getting trains to run on time. Getting enough people on to trains and home in time for dinner, TV, feet-up, ravioli.

OCTOPUS

I'm trying to work out if complete happiness is achieved when nothing is asked of me, or if it's the flipside of all that and when I'm asked to give it everything I've got.

LIGHT

In about 50 years' time there will be facilities that will allow the birthday cake to be beamed from yours to mine – the cake turned into a picture and lifted up in a stream of pixel by pixel... Then two seconds later turned back into cream, slab and crumbs again, or maybe half-crumbs, half-picture if it's a kind of surprise party with films, oil screens and projectors.

RAIN

There was no official name for rain for a long time – it just started falling and folk let it get on with the job. It possibly was named when kids said for the first time ever, 'tell us the story about Chicken Licken and his bad leg'. This happened and the rain kept falling. Someone tried to describe it, saying, part melon, part cockroach, part soup tureen. But it was no use and the rain just kept on coming and still does till this day.

FIRE

Fire just does what it does. For example, put a rag on fire into a wasps' nest and see what happens. Mr Half-Dead thought that black seething mass was the jam he was saving for Christmas. Fire just does what it does.

ISTANBUL

I thought Istanbul was all cat meat, flies and hair oil; it was fake gold watches and street children shaking their fists and selling pens. I got there and saw the Blue Mosque with a handful of seagulls coasting over it at five a.m. which makes it look more like the Blue Mosque in a fairy story, and that makes the cats and flies and hair oil, the watches and the children with their pens like something in a fairy story too.

ANXIETY

It's like my ideas give me vertigo – the minute I lie down the room pitches this way and that. It's like my ideas make me seasick, or they're chock-full of sinking sand. The moment I strike out one way my ideas head off in the other. I throw my hands up and say enough is enough but my ideas have other ideas and say let's get some hamburgers. I'm firm on this, and I say we are meant to be vegetarian, but my ideas just laugh and pour out ketchup.

LUCK

So I woke up and you gave me a good idea: taken off the side of a rock, cobbled together from two random dreams – who can say? Then I went back to sleep and you took it away again – stuck it back on the side of the rock; tucked it back into the dreams – your weird playfellows.

SAPPHIRE

No matter if you box it up in a museum, or whatever –
the sapphire just rocks back and considers all the words
it knows: *fork* and *cake*, and *anonymous*. Even *determined*.
Restraining order, too, and *final demand*... A clever sapphire
...

TV

The inventors of the TV desperate to tune into lying
with the tiger in his dark green hole with a second set of
shadowy stripes playing across the real ones on his back.
All of those channels, quickly snapping through them and
still no joy, but still time, still time.

HORMONES

Hormones are best kept in glass jars, or vials – keeping them straight and upright like soldiers on a battlefield, or maybe even more like the tall thin reeds at the side of a battlefield. While everyone scrabbles for rations and horses' heads get blown off – and the whole world is generally turned to grey chopped slop – hormones are kept high, thin and proud, the last things standing.

ICELAND

Twenty-nine cool-air radio channels and a deer on a hill that is just a minuscule speck of red. A horse on a hill, too, that's just a tiny dot of black, and then all the houses – tiny specks of white – in the backdraft of cold-air radio channel, fish breath, the little airport's tiny black speckle, the rock pools.

CARTOONIST

I suppose I hang around thinking hard about train time-tables and meeting folk in mountain resorts and bra clips and pork chops. I think about that stuff all afternoon – till the coffee is cold and a mountain resort is just a long list of numbers, and a timetable a speck of snow. A pork chop is a clip and a bra a plastic laser beam. Then the paper comes out and I draw a face.

WATER

We opened the well lid and the water looked deep into our faces like it knew something magnificent about every one of us.

SHADOWS

Just when we didn't need any more chimeras and mysteries, shadows came along. You position yourself with the expensive binoculars at 200 feet, focusing intently on the frosted glass, the net curtain, the mirror-back. 'Are they into draughts?' you ask, 'or what about the Amazon rain forest?' No – that's just you – a reflection of yourself.

.

HOMESICKNESS

If you think about homesickness long enough – intensely, single-pointedly – then sometimes it comes out as moustache oil, and sometimes lumps of apple pie. At other times, white starched bed sheets, or maybe 'I offer to you now this whole village.' But most of all, five times more than all the other stuff, it's face–cup–kiss.

GRASSHOPPER

It's an interesting thought that the first tank makers based their tanks around the grasshopper – its angles and plates set around a tight, tough, pristine centre point. They couldn't get the legs right, though, and stuck fat ugly tracks on instead, and the grasshopper kicked clear.

KNIFE

So your sugary little crystal sits on the edge, or does the edge sit on your sugary little crystal?

DUST MOTES

Dust motes' gold and blue glamour-lustre not the best thing – that's the endless cycle of them thinking about sweetening tea with jam, the funny spectacle of balancing a plate on a spoon.

JEALOUSY

The jealousy that we know of now is far more potent that the stuff found in the olden days, or even in fairy tales. It's not as if the jealousy of bygone eras and books could be siphoned off and used to power a big city like Tokyo, which it could, today.

HEARTBREAK

The great thing about heartbreak is that it likes to think it's not heartbroken, but just playing up to heartbroken – acting the way it's meant to act. The whole thing is like it's on stage, and it's the director, the stagehand, the runner, and also the writer. It's costume design, too, and the grey-lipped dramaturg hanging out from the wings shouting, whoa!, and, you're doing great!

FLY

It's not like the fly just flicks open its eyes and the room is all there: far from it. More like a mental mapping of things – lengths and depths; ratios; nothing left to chance; a bit-by-bit scanning. It not like it goes around wearing a t-shirt that says, 'The Mermaid Made Me Do It': more like Moby Dick, or the depth charge; submarines.

SAND

They say, so what came first, the egg or sand? And most say, well it's the egg. But then what did the egg use to get its foot up? (And what about the bit of grit that causes all the commotion?)

LION

Well, say you are looking over the 600 final proposals for an energy-efficient light bulb, or for the new flyover, and you take away the weakest one: that's what the lion does.

SURGERY

Surgery is no better than the writing life, is no better than a dog's life, is no better than a puff of air: now, where did I put that cotton ball?

RADIO WAVES

The radio wasn't devised in Scotland – that was just the fine-tuning of it. The radio was a long time before that: when the spider behind the cooker used to do nothing except read books, and then all those written along the inside of a leg. His mother, too, knitting pompoms from fallen leaves and those all scratchy as hell. But it wasn't as if the radio at this point was a fiction; already mother'd switch it on and listen in to the horse racing.

BUTTER

Chess in the hills is where it all started: the maestro with their seventeen moves planned in advance goes up against the novice. The novice says, 'my tiny mind is turning to butter.' 'What's butter?' Then they came off the hill and didn't play chess for about seven full weeks.

OXYGEN

Well, I just want you to know that I haven't thought about you for even a single minute today – *not even a single minute* – and I hope you are pleased with yourself.

ADDICTION

They say things like, 'who's the one in the reeking house-coat?' and, 'what creep's got to climb over the 20,000 fag douts scattered up outside this front door?' But neither of these is me. I'm actually as clear as a polished empty glass bottle, and I don't even drink.

FORGETFULNESS

Doesn't even remember to put down its lever arch file and assortment of papers when it's getting passionately kissed in the secret broom cupboard, and only remembers years later when it's married with six kids.

SLEEP

Sleep – well that comes with its own brand of paralysis so you don't act out your dreams: turning into the old tyrant with the accordion; trying to catch the full force of 1500 Fahrenheit exhaust gases blasted from four RB211 Rolls-Royce turbines in a hair net. Sure, sleep definitely has its functions and its place.

BLUEBEARD

The only thing worse than finding a fly in the pickled cabbage – not finding a fly in the pickled cabbage.

MINNEAPOLIS

Knickerbocker glory; pecan ruffle bite; banana split; Min-
neapolis: *haha* – that city's only playing at car factories,
grey depots and a crummy small to medium sized zoo.

WEDDING

Things can get a bit cosy and cookie up at the altar – the bit the big pronouncements are made. All that's because chance has had a sizeable part to play, and that makes folk a little giddy. Not far off going up the park and sitting beside that woman pulling things out of her capacious handbag: a stapler; an ice-cube maker; a snow suit; a bikini. Then it's, that's just what I was looking for! and, how did you know?, and you're giddy with it.

FASHION

The first fashion coming in with the Era of Birds – the one that nearly slipped between all the others, but not quite. That time when sewing and fashion became the big things; folk getting the garments really good, and having a few looks at themselves in the pot hanging beside the fire. That reflection no better than a bird looking at a reflection of itself in a grimy puddle, but the garments were perfect, like feathers.

TATTOO

He says, I want to write a story that's more like a tattoo. He says it again down by the wagon that sells the candied scorpions, and, as if reminded, later again by the man in the bloody apron and the vats of scorpion fudge.

SANTIAGO

Mama said, let's move to Santiago, and we did. The build-
ings were close together making that city very dark, but
the electric whiteness of tornado lollies and ice-cream
eyeballs made up for it, and amongst that darkness was
the first place they found night owls.

ACKNOWLEDGEMENTS

A huge heartfelt thank you to Fred Hannah, Keith Patterson, Gerry Cambridge, Graham Smith, Mel Grossman, Jim Carruth, Elizabeth Brown, Jim McIvor, Eric Judlin, Alice Forbes, Hazel Frew and Christie Williamson. So too, a big beam of love sent out to dear Sandy Hutchison.

Some of these poems, or versions, have appeared in *The Dark Horse*, *Gutter*, *New Writing Scotland 33* and *Northwords Now*. 'Netball' was a commission for Glasgow's Commonwealth Games and was published in *The Laws of the Game* and featured in a poster campaign at the Tron Theatre.